Your Wealth*Confidence* Scorecard

Discover the 8 Mindsets Necessary to Live Better Now

Thomas L. Kirk

Your Wealth*Confidence* Scorecard

Printed by:
90-Minute Books
302 Martinique Drive
Winter Haven, FL 33884
www.90minutebooks.com

Published in the United States of America

Book ID: 160715-00468

ISBN-13: 978-1945733048
ISBN-10: 1945733047

For more information on 90-Minute Books including finding out how you can publish your own lead generating book, visit 90minutebooks.com or call (863) 318-0464

Here's What's Inside...

Introduction

I used to think that once someone had money they would stop worrying about it. What I've found over the years is that it's less about how much money you have, and more how you think about money.

My friend Dan Sullivan says the problem isn't the problem, the problem is you don't know how to think about the problem. Most of the time, people are making decisions about their wealth in isloated silos. They save a certain amount of money, they try to pay off their debt, they have kids they want to put through college, they have an idea about when they want to retire; they're really hoping it all works out. But deep down inside, they are afraid it may not. They don't have a process or structure to use so that each of their decisions support and reinforce each other, moving them closer and closer to the financial future they have in mind for themselves.

If you listen to the general narrative about all the problems in the world, especially about economics and your money, taxes, investing and the volatility of it all, it's easy to have a low Wealth*Confidence* Score. When you have low confidence about your money it filters your perception of everything that's going on in your life. When someone is constantly worried about their money they don't enjoy all the wealth that they have available to them, which includes things other than just money. It includes things like relationships and where you choose to live. It includes your physical health and your hobbies. It's easy to get so distracted by what *may* happen that you go through life without even being aware of it. I am passionate about helping people recognize what they can control, taking steps to manage that, and increase their Wealth*Confidence* Score so they can better enjoy the abundance in their lives.

Enjoy the book!

I hope this book educates you on the actions you can take to live a more abundant life with improved peace of mind and improved Wealth*Confidence*. I hope it inspires you to stay focused on your individual Wealth*Plan*™ and not let all the noise of the world distract you.

To Your Abundant Future!

Thomas L. Kirk

Mindset Number One: Grateful

In column number one, you may feel sorry for yourself because **you don't have enough of what you want and need**. Instead of being grateful, this can leave you angry or envious.

In column two, **your hard work has not been appropriately rewarded by the world.** You're attempting to do what you feel is necessary to get what you need, but it's just not working. This can be very irritating.

In column three, you do experience times of being grateful, because **you measure your level of success by comparing it to that of others**. This leaves you feeling comfortable and maybe even a little superior to the others with whom you compare yourself.

In column four, **you appreciate the success you have achieved and look forward to still more.** When you reflect back on your life, you see how everything that happened contributed to where you are right now and are amazed at how it all fit together.

You may not appreciate what you already have, because you don't know how far along you have already come. To improve your score in this area, begin by benchmarking where you are now.

This would include your assets, liabilities, income, and expense.

The result of this effort often surprises people. The total at the bottom of a series of numbers always seems to be larger than you think it will be. This happens almost every time I pay the bill at a restaurant. How can a traditional breakfast of eggs, potatoes, toast, coffee, plus a tip, add up to over $20 for just two people? But it does.

The same thing can happen when you make a list that contains the savings accounts, retirement plan balances, property investments, and other assets you have accumulated over your years of hard work. Each one of these balances may not be that large in isolation, but when you add them together, you may find that you are the millionaire next door and didn't even know it.

When you know what you have now, you can be much more excited about what is possible. You begin to understand how the life you dream about is within reach, and your Wealth*Confidence* Score improves.

Mindset Number Two: Open-Minded

In column one, **you rely on your highly developed survival skills to succeed in this challenging world.** Those survival skills include your mental and physical strength.

In column two, you want to be open-minded but **you often feel overwhelmed by today's complexities.** This can leave you exhausted as more and more keeps getting thrown at you.

In column three, **you have the answers to most questions.** You have a well-rounded base of knowledge.   When people have questions, you usually have a point of view that needs to be shared. This makes you feel respected and admired for what you know.

In column four, **you comprehend complex issues, relationships, and appreciate new ideas**. The exponential expansion of the body of knowledge and its increasing ease of access is exciting and empowering to you.

With so much information at our fingertips today, much of it can appear to contradict itself. Buy stocks, sell stocks, have debt, have no debt, all at the same time. How are you to decide?

In his groundbreaking book, *The Paradox of Choice - Why More Is Less*, Barry Schwartz describes how whether we're buying a pair of jeans, ordering a cup of coffee, selecting a long-distance carrier, applying to college, choosing a doctor, or setting up a 401K, everyday decisions, both big and small, have become increasingly complex due to the overwhelming abundance of choices with which we are presented. In the long run, this can lead to decision-making paralysis, anxiety, and perpetual stress. In a culture that tells us that there is no excuse for falling short of perfection when your options are limitless, too much choice can lead to clinical depression. This is not good for Your Wealth*Confidence*.

To improve your score in this area, you must be able to put these choices into the context of your individual situation, goals, and aspirations. Answer the following questions: What do you have now? What will you need to create the financial life you dream of? What actions can you take now to move toward that future? Answers to these questions will help you look at the various choices you have, in light of individual and collective contributions to your vision of your future.

This helps avoid the problem of contempt before investigation. Instead of classifying an idea or strategy as being good or bad, decide whether it contributes positively or negatively to the future you have in mind.

Determining if the decision contributes or detracts from your financial future takes time and can be found by monitoring your progress over time. By comparing how the growth of your financial resources is progressing towards what you will need helps determine what you must do next. Once you know this, it's much easier to make your decisions, monitor your progress, adjust your course and improve Your Wealth*Confidence.*

Mindset Number Three: Cooperative

In column one, **you see your way as the best way and that more people should just think like you do.** You feel the world would run much better if more people lived, thought and acted just like you do.

In column two, **you reluctantly work with others but expect that they will let you down**. This feeling is based on past experiences that you've had and conversations with others.

In column three, **you see working with others as necessary to accomplish your goals**. In this way, you see cooperation as the lesser of two evils. One evil is you don't get your way, the other evil is you have to work with others in order to get your way. It's a lesser of these two evils to be cooperative.

In column four, **you enjoy collaborative relationships with other open-minded and grateful people.** When part of such a team, you feel that everyone is better off than anyone would have been on their own.

It's entertaining to think you can do all that is necessary to create the financial life you dream of, all on your own. There are so many tools you can use to try to do this; TurboTax, discounted brokerage and portfolio management, LegalZoom, Rocket Mortgage. This idea is very attractive because it's hard to find and then manage the relationships with professionals you might use instead of these do-it-yourself solutions. The more attention you give to these topics (income tax, estate tax, portfolio design, risk management, retirement planning, etc.) the more you realize what you don't know. If you don't know what you don't know, the result can be disastrous.

Just the other day, I heard a radio advertisement for an online service that offers to help you create your own corporation or LLC. The main reason they gave why someone should do this, was to avail themselves of the liability shield such structures can provide, which is true. They said they do not provide legal or accounting advice, just incorporation assistance.

But there are additional actions necessary for this liability protection to stand up when a lawsuit arises. My attorney friends call these additional actions the formalities of corporate existence. These include annual shareholder meetings, separate books and records, proper state regulatory filings, etc. If your corporation is sued, and you are missing these actions, a prosecuting attorney may be able to pierce the corporate veil, subjecting your personal asset to judgment from the court. This is exactly what you were trying to avoid when you incorporated online.

What is needed to improve your score in this area is an independent team manager to help you coordinate and integrate the advice you are getting. This helps you to identify and retain the resources you require, then integrate the advice you receive into your overall Wealth*Plan*™. The sometimes conflicting advice from lawyers, accountants, bankers, insurance agents, and realtors, etc., can be coordinated to support your continuing progress.

There is a word of warning; be sure you're aware of any possible conflicts of interest that can arise through receipts of referral fees, commissions, and proprietary in-house financial products. For this to work at increasing your score in this area, your independent manager should be your financial advocate, and place your interest above all others.

The positive results from this include simplification and balance; simplification is the orderly control of all the important financial details of your life, and balance, where each of these financial decisions supports or reinforces each other, and increased Wealth*Confidence*.

Mindset Number Four: Respectful

In column one, **you are a strong communicator, making sure your point of view is understood**. You are comfortable stating your position two or three times if necessary in a conversation with others, to be sure your point of view is known.

In column two, **you feel duty-bound to inject your thoughts and opinions where they are needed**. Sometimes, even when you don't have a dog in the fight, you feel if you have an opinion to share, it needs to be shared.

In column three, **you treat others with the same level of respect with which they treat you**. Here you see respect of others as a quid pro quo, in that respect given is the same as respect received.

In column four, **you are not easily offended, and can learn from differing ideas and points of view**. You recognized that your thinking is perspective and experience dependent and can understand why someone may think differently from another vantage point.

In the cacophony of opinions and ideas in the marketplace, it can seem like only the ones that are expressed the loudest will be the ones heard and respected, so you follow suit. What can happen, is while you're waiting for the briefest of moments to interject, you completely miss valuable information that you could use because you are so focused on being sure your voice is heard.

Most people hate being sold, I know I do. It doesn't matter if it's a used car, a piece of jewelry, or life insurance. The sales process often has a common attribute; the sales person does all the talking, all about them, all about their product, all about why you need to buy what is being sold. This is understandable since they only get paid if you buy something, but it can leave you wondering if you made the best decision.

Your Wealth*Plan*™ should start by asking about the vision you have of your financial life and your tangible financial goals, the accomplishments of which would make you feel like you're progressing toward your future. Only then can the usefulness of particular strategies and actions be determined and implemented.

Your ideas and opinions have been sought as a foundation from the beginning. Suggested actions are not offensive but instead are understood as steps you must take to create the future you have in mind, increasing Your Wealth*Confidence*.

Mindset Number Five: Abundance

In column one, **you see most resources running out and you are hunkering down to protect what you have**. You see the world primarily as a zero sum game, that somebody's win is at the cost of somebody's loss, and that as a total, it's a zero sum.

In column two, **you feel that the best is behind us and little can be done to bring it back**. You find yourself often wishing for the good old days.

In column three, **you see things as good now but not getting much better**, so you feel you may as well relax and enjoy the current situation because this is as good as it's going to get.

In column four, **you see most things getting better and look forward to being part of that exciting future.** You see human ingenuity as the most important natural resource and it growing in leaps and bounds.

It's one thing to be aware of what is happening in the world around us, and quite another to let fear cloud everything we do. If you listen to the headlines, it's too easy to get sucked into perpetual fear. Yet, if we look around at our individual situations, we find that we have it pretty good, in some cases very good. Those fearful headlines can overshadow the enjoyment of all the wealth in our lives that includes more than just money; our family, health, living conditions, leisure activities, etc.

I have friends who are financially independent and no longer work, after having long, successful careers. During their working years, they were often legitimately furious about the amount of income taxes they had to pay. They would still sometimes express annoyance at the increasing income taxes on our land, worried that the government would take yet more of their hard-earned wealth. This was until I reminded them that since they are now living off their investments, and no longer have wages as income, they are not subject to these increased tax rates at all. While the taxes may, in fact, be higher, these higher rates don't apply to them and all the time and worry they wasted on this problem was unnecessary.

My friend Dan Sullivan calls this the general versus specific narrative.

The general narrative is everything is going to hell; such as taxes are going up. The specific narrative is what's happening in your specific life; these high rates don't apply to you. Since we are constantly bombarded by the general narrative, it can completely color our perception of the abundance in our specific lives; being financially dependent and no longer needing to work.

The process contained in my book, 'Are You Worried About Your Money?' helps you to focus on your specific narrative, to develop and implement the strategies and actions to magnify that and better enjoy all you have worked so hard to accomplish.

Mindset Number Six:
Connected

In column one, **you are a rugged individualist who has few relationships with other people**. You can be alone even in a crowded room.

In column two, **you find it difficult to be transparent and genuine with others**. You find yourself searching and hoping for a change in this area, but are frustrated by your slow progress.

In column three, **you know a lot of people but very few with whom you can confide**, yet you are comfortable with that level of connection.

In column four, **you surround yourself with others who you share a mutual trust and respect**. You rely on an appropriate level of inter-dependence these kind of relationships can support.

How can people have 500 Facebook friends and still feel isolated? It's easy. Digital communication can increase our reach far beyond what was ever possible before, but can also dehumanize the relationships we have with others. The quantity of the relationships can replace their quality.

We can be so distracted by all the noise, that we don't have time to pursue all the relationships, even if we wanted to. I have friends and family who have stopped using some of the most popular social media platforms, and they say they don't miss it. They also say the experience has improved their state of mind and feeling of well-being as a result. They are no longer distracted by the constant banter about where someone ate lunch, startled cat videos, or peoples' political view that they don't care to hear about.

We can't go into hibernation. We are social creatures. How are you to improve your score in this area? One way is to find a private Wealth*Coach*™ with whom you can share your individual situation, dreams, and aspirations.

Since the creation of the future you dream of doesn't happen overnight, you will likely be working together for years. Through careful management and periodic updates of your strategies and actions, you will see how they work together to help create the future you have in mind. The connection to your Wealth*Coach*™ is like that of oxen, equally yoked, pulling the plow in the same direction, making progress together that could not be achieved by them individually.

Mindset Number Seven: Optimistic

In column one, **you see your contribution to most situations as being the devil's advocate**. You don't want enthusiasm to get too carried away in any particular area.

In column two, **you find yourself focusing more on what's going wrong than on what is going right**, and since what you focus on gets bigger, you can waste a lot of energy on things that may or may not happen.

In column three, **you are optimistic in good times but pessimistic in bad times**. Since life throws curve balls at different times, your optimism is easily swayed back and forth.

In column four, **you usually find the silver lining even in those things that are hard to understand**. You have experienced when good has come from the most challenging of circumstances. This gives you hope when it happens again.

I have found that when circumstances happen, I immediately jump to conclusions about whether it's a good thing or a bad thing that just happened, only to find out in hindsight that my call about being good or bad was completely wrong.

Here's an example. I started out in college with the intention of becoming a doctor but bombed chemistry, a very bad thing at the time. My dad was a doctor, I was the first born son, thus there was a lot of momentum behind me becoming a doctor. Here I was in my second year of college and needing to find a different field of study. I chose accounting. No one in my family was an accountant; I didn't know what accounting involved or what accountants did.

Because I bombed chemistry, I met my wife of 34 years at the accounting firm where I started after I graduated. I founded a CPA firm, and a wealth management company, to help people make smart decisions about their money, and have had a fabulous career and a great time. Bombing chemistry turned out to be a very good thing after all.

The point here is that it's often difficult to tell what is good or bad, in the moment of something happening to you. This can happen with your finances, too. Bad things can and do happen to your personal financial situation. If you have a Wealth*Plan*™, based on everything you know at the time, you are better able to adjust your future strategies and actions in response to your new set of circumstances.

You lose your job, a bad thing, but because you have a Wealth*Plan*™ you know how long you can search for your next job, how much you need to make to stay on track, and where you're going to get the cash flow to live on in the meantime.

Having a Wealth*Plan*™ can increase your score in this area. That way, when life throws you a curve ball, you'll have a better idea about the effect it will have on your ability to stay on course, respond creatively, and be more optimistic about what comes next.

Mindset Number Eight: Realistic

In column one, **you are frustrated by unmet demands in a world that is unfair**. This can leave you depressed and demoralized.

In column two, **you attempt to control future events and accept things only when that doesn't work**. Since you try to control things that are uncontrollable, you end up wasting a lot of energy.

In column three, **your expectations of people, places, and things often exceed actual behavior and events**. In defense, you lower your expectations to avoid this frustration.

In column four, **you accept life on life's terms and adjust your attitudes and actions to live in peace**. You recognize the ebb and flow of life; good and bad times; easy and hard days. Not letting any of them steal your joy of living.

Some people say that expectations are the yardstick of disappointments. I think this is only true of unrealistic expectations. If Your Wealth*Confidence* is dependent on you winning the lottery, or making 15% in a return every year on your money, you're going to be disappointed because these are unrealistic.

A version of the serenity prayer written in 1932 by American theologian Reinhold Niebuhr says, "God, grant us the serenity to accept the things we cannot change, courage to change the things we can, and wisdom to know the difference."

While there are things about the financial world you cannot control, there are plenty you can. You can invest your money in a low-cost, globally diversified portfolio to help capture market returns instead of gambling with it, through market timing or concentrated investing. You can develop the discipline of saving on a regular basis and not use high-interest rate debt. You can avoid conspicuous consumption, and instead allow compound interest to exponentially magnify your pile of money, so you will one day have what you need to stop working, if you so desire.

If you are more realistic about your expectations as to income, investment returns, living expenses, how long you plan to work, etc., your expected future results will be more accurate and your likelihood of achieving them will be increased. You'll be able to make decisions confident about the effect they will have on your future, increasing Your Wealth*Confidence* Score.

Here's what to do next...

To continue to improve Your Wealth*Confidence* Scorecard results, here are three ways you can take your thinking to the next level.

1 Download 'Are You Worried About Your Money?' for free at **www.FirstWaveFinancial.com.**

2 Watch the introduction video on our website where I describe the mindsets necessary for improved Wealth*Confidence* in more detail.

3 Schedule your free consultation with one of our Wealth*Coaches*, where we walk through the initial steps you can take right now to increase Your Wealth*Confidence* Score, at **info@FirstWaveFinancial.com.**

Get started now at
www.FirstWaveFinancial.com

Your Wealth*Confidence* Scorecard

While looking at each column, see which one of the four descriptions of the particular mindset resonates with you. Then, decide how much it describes you by your number score. A five would indicate that column describes you pretty well, six might mean you are in that column but almost in the next column. You can easily see what will contribute to a higher score by reading the description of the column to the right of your score. Score yourself twice for each mindset, once for how you see yourself right now, and once as a goal for how you'd like yourself to be. There's also space for you to add comments or notes to capture your thinking, as you consider your mindset.

This assessment offers a quantitative view of the quality of Your Wealth*Confidence*. It not only shows the mindset that you are fully experiencing now, by your high score, but also those where you may be struggling now, by your low score, and those where the most improvement is possible by the spread between your current score and your goal score. This book contains suggested actions you can take to either help bridge the gap between where you are and where you want to be, or to maintain your already high score.

Mindset: Grateful	
You don't have enough of what you want and need.	1
	2
	3
Your hard work has not been appropriately rewarded by the world.	4
	5
	6
You measure your level of success by comparing it to that of others.	7
	8
	9
You appreciate the success you have achieved and look forward to still more.	**10**
	11
	12

How would you rate yourself, on a scale of 1-12?	
What is your ideal goal, on a scale of 1-12?	

Insights and Actions:

Mindset: Open-Minded	
You rely on highly developed survival skills to succeed in this challenging world.	1
	2
	3
You often feel overwhelmed by today's complexities.	4
	5
	6
You have an answer to most questions.	7
	8
	9
You comprehend complex issues and relationships and appreciate new ideas.	10
	11
	12

How would you rate yourself, on a scale of 1-12?	
What is your ideal goal, on a scale of 1-12?	

Insights and Actions:

Mindset: Cooperative	
You see your way as the best way and that more people should think like you do.	1
	2
	3
You reluctantly work with others but expect they will let you down.	4
	5
	6
You see working with others as necessary to accomplish your goals.	7
	8
	9
You enjoy collaborative relationships with other open-minded, grateful people.	10
	11
	12

How would you rate yourself, on a scale of 1-12?	
What is your ideal goal, on a scale of 1-12?	

Insights and Actions:

Mindset: Respectful	
You are a strong communicator, making sure your point of view is understood.	1
	2
	3
You feel duty-bound to interject your thoughts and opinions where they are needed.	4
	5
	6
You treat others with the same level of respect with which they treat you.	7
	8
	9
You are not easily offended and can learn from differing ideas and points of view.	10
	11
	12

How would you rate yourself, on a scale of 1-12?	
What is your ideal goal, on a scale of 1-12?	

Insights and Actions:

Mindset: Abundance	
You see most things running out and are hunkering down to protect what you have.	1
	2
	3
You feel the best is behind us and little can be done to bring it back.	4
	5
	6
You see things as good now, but probably not getting much better.	7
	8
	9
You see most things getting better and look forward to being part of that exciting future.	10
	11
	12

How would you rate yourself, on a scale of 1-12?	
What is your ideal goal, on a scale of 1-12?	

Insights and Actions:

Mindset: Connected	
You are a rugged individualist who has few relationships with other people.	**1**
	2
	3
You find it difficult to be transparent and genuine with others.	**4**
	5
	6
You know a lot of people, but very few with whom you feel you can confide.	**7**
	8
	9
You surround yourself with others with whom you share mutual trust and respect.	**10**
	11
	12

How would you rate yourself, on a scale of 1-12?	
What is your ideal goal, on a scale of 1-12?	

Insights and Actions:

Mindset: Optimistic	
You see your contribution to most situations as being the "devil's advocate".	1
	2
	3
You find yourself focusing more on what is going wrong than on what is going right.	4
	5
	6
You are optimistic in good times and pessimistic in bad times.	7
	8
	9
You usually find the "silver lining", even in those things that are hard to understand.	10
	11
	12

How would you rate yourself, on a scale of 1-12?	
What is your ideal goal, on a scale of 1-12?	

Insights and Actions:

Mindset: Realistic	
You are frustrated by unmet demands in a world that is basically unfair.	1
	2
	3
You attempt to control future events and accept things only when that doesn't work.	4
	5
	6
Your expectations of people, places and things often exceed actual behavior and events.	7
	8
	9
You accept life on life's terms and adjust your attitudes and actions to live in peace.	10
	11
	12

How would you rate yourself, on a scale of 1-12?	
What is your ideal goal, on a scale of 1-12?	

Insights and Actions:

Your Wealth*Confidence* Scorecard

Mindsets	Score	Goal
Grateful		
Open-Minded		
Cooperative		
Respectful		
Abundance		
Connected		
Optimistic		
Realistic		

Total Scores:		

IMPORTANT DISCLOSURE INFORMATION

PLEASE NOTE: MATERIAL LIMITATIONS. Different types of investments involve varying degrees of risk. Therefore, it should not be assumed that future performance of any specific investment or investment strategy (including the investments and/or investment strategies referenced in this book or recommended or undertaken by FirstWave Financial) or any other investment-related or financial planning content, will be profitable, equal any corresponding indicated historical performance level(s), be suitable or appropriate for a reader's individual situation, or prove successful. Moreover, no portion of the book content should be construed as a substitute for individual investment and/or financial planning advice from the financial professional(s) of a reader's choosing, including Mr. Kirk or other members of FirstWave Financial. The author, Thomas Kirk, provides advisory services solely in his capacity as a Wealth*Coach*™ of FirstWave Financial, a registered investment adviser located in Satellite Beach, Florida. As such, this book is not, and is not intended to serve as, a substitute for individual advice from Mr. Kirk or any member of FirstWave Financial. No reader should construe that any discussion in the book of actual client experiences serves as any indication or assurance that an existing or prospective client will experience a certain level of results if FirstWave Financial is engaged, or continues to be engaged to provide investment advisory services. A copy of FirstWave Financial's current written disclosure statement discussing its advisory services and fees is available upon request. ANY QUESTIONS: Regarding the above limitations, FirstWave Financial's Chief Compliance Officer, Laura K. Chiesman, CFP®, remains available to address them.